I0883934

The Burning World

ALSO BY ROBERT GIBB

The Names of the Earth in Summer

The Winter House

Momentary Days

Fugue for a Late Snow

The Origins of Evening

The Burning World

poems by

ROBERT GIBB

THE UNIVERSITY OF
ARKANSAS PRESS

Fayetteville

2004

Copyright © 2004 by The University of Arkansas Press

All rights reserved
Manufactured in the United States of America

08 07 06 05 04 5 4 3 2 1

Designed by Liz Lester

⊗ The paper used in this publication meets the minimum requirements of the American National Standard for Permanence of Paper for Printed Library Materials Z39.48-1984.

LIBRARY OF CONGRESS
CATALOGING-IN-PUBLICATION DATA

Gibb, Robert.
The burning world : poems / by Robert Gibb.
p. cm.
ISBN 1-55728-765-1 (pbk. : alk. paper)
I. Title.
PS3557.I139B87 2004
811'.54—dc22 2003018576

ACKNOWLEDGMENTS

American Literary Review: "Ash and Stone"; *Arts & Letters:* "Cigar: An Ode," "Folding the Fox"; *The Kenyon Review*: "Pictures at an Exhibition"; *The Laurel Review:* "A Memorium for the Syria Mosque Razed to Make Space for Parking"; *Hiram Poetry Review:* "Homestead Park"; *Manoa:* "A Poem Written for the Aviary at the Time of Its Possible Closing," "The Jars"; *Margie:* "Rust Belt" (as "*Gregory's Scrapping*"); *The Missouri Review:* "Sifting through the Remains," "Lost Waters," "The Employments of Time in Homestead," "Magnetic North," "First Visit to My Mother's Grave, North Side Catholic Cemetery"; *Poetry:* "Quatrains for a Christmas Bear"; *Poetry East:* "In the Emergency Room," "Brain Coral," "Salvation Army"; *Shenandoah:* "Martha in Darkness"; *The Southern Review:* "Lewis Hine: Two Photographs," "Steel Engravings," "Phipps Conservatory," "The Burning World"; *The Widener Review:* "For the Inmate Pedro Velázquez, Who Restored a Wooden Tricycle for Our Youngest Son's Christmas"

An earlier version of "Homestead Park" appeared in the 1984 *Anthology of Magazine Verse & Yearbook of American Poetry.*

"For the Inmate Pedro Velázquez, Who Restored a Wooden Tricycle for Our Youngest Son's Christmas" appeared in the 1986–87 *Anthology of Magazine Verse & Yearbook of American Poetry.*

"Folding the Fox" appeared in *Pushcart Prize XXV: The Best of the Small Presses.*

Acknowledgement, and thanks, is also due the National Endowment for the Arts, a grant from whom was crucial in the completion of this book.

for Maggie

CONTENTS

The Burning World

I

A fire as cold and slow as rusting metal

—ANTHONY HECHT

Pictures at an Exhibition

PITTSBURGH Revealed
Photographs Since 1850

1. ***River View with Barges.***
Hew Charles Torrance, 1924

Not quite *fin de siècle,* this twilight,
The city lost in haze behind the massed flats,
The river a molten mirror on which light
Has been laved.
Coal hoist and smokestacks.
The spidery fretwork of bridges
Like shapes in the rain, the solvent
Of that climate, their girders smudged.

"Hell with the lid off," people referred to it,
But this is fit for a jeweler's scale—
The black smoke of the tugboat and white smoke
Of the train, the barges converging like rails—
A world faintly blurred, as if seismic.

Gelatin silver, not oxides. Not the leachings
Of metal, but a river of burnished shale.

2. ***USS Homestead Works and Neighborhood.***
W. Eugene Smith, 1955–57

From the vantage of Seventh Avenue
And Amity Street: a palimpsest

Set in time. The vault of the steel mill flattened
And walling up space, distances compressed.

Beneath a gray strip of sky the first shift's over,
Traffic threaded across both sets of tracks.
Shirt-sleeved men on the sidewalks.
That shingle for PONZIE'S CAFE the focal
Point of the photograph.
                                        He can't have stopped
The light down much before it, checking
Lens and meter across from my father's office,
His "long poem called Pittsburgh" coalescing.

Now, he could see from there clear across the river
To the trash trees flashing on the farther shore.

3. *Old Money.* **Duane Michals, 1978**

FRICK, SCAIFE, JONES, DRAVO, OLIVER, and HORNE—
Like a drum roll from *Paradise Lost!* Flesh made words
Cut squarely into marble, each grave frontal
And framed, each as monumental
As you'd expect.
                              Even for them celebrity's
Meant aging in public, shapes of light
Fallen among metals and their chiseled names.
Proximate like this, the tombs seem interchangeable,
Variations on a theme so obvious

It's unaccompanied by any text.

Unlike the tribute to Michals's own family
Posed before the ruins of the Duquesne mills—
Now we are all gone—
                                        no sparked flames arcing
Or angels spreading their slow stone wings.

In the Emergency Room

My son at four months old had lungs
That flared up on the X-rays like spectral stones,
Tablets upon which dark moss was growing.

So we bundled him in to Sacred Heart
And sat huddled in the emergency room, praying
The small fronds of his breathing would loosen

Into light. Outside, the gray sides of buildings
Gradually became the gray lengths of dusk
Filling the city—a half-tone darkening upward

As it emptied into the whole of the winter night.
And so it seemed to me still, watching an intern
Cover the flesh of our son with his stethoscope's

Cold eclipse. Small, naked, without words,
The child cried out his panic, while I,
With no words but love's helplessness and anger,

Stumbled and drew nearer that body, close
To the distances it traveled, through bone
And broken water, to be delivered into this life.

All the while, from beyond us, I could hear
Someone muttering, *"I don't know . . . six drinks,*
Seven, maybe eight." And the doctor pleading,

"How can we help if you won't listen to us?
You know you're killing yourself." And then
Our intern, explaining how viruses curdle

The cells, "But he'll be fine, just see that he
Takes these," restoring us to our ordinary worries.
With my wife gone to fill out forms,

I gathered up the blankets and baby things
And started to leave for the car. Which is when
I saw him, splayed on the table before me,

The soles of his feet yellow and soiled
With earth as in Mantegna's painting of Christ's
Foreshortened corpse—although these legs,

Uncovered, were almost violet in their mantle
Of veins, the color of home-made wine.
I wondered how it was with him

Whose death was a shimmering cup, and pain
Something I might only hope to guess at,
Having come myself only so close to the bone.

Brain Coral

Lopped and stalky as cauliflower,
The coral lay on the hearth, full-blown,

A burl from the reef, dry as bisqueware.
It filled my hands,

The calcium scraping my knuckles
Those hours I sat unlodging

The wedged bodies from their crevices,
Lining them up on the tiles:

A scaled-down flotilla
Of tiny, salmon-colored shells,

Ghostly bones and augers
Adding their fathoms to the room.

And if I thought of them as shipwrecked
Or surfacing things

Flung up from the coral, I'd been taught
The whole world rose from flood.

Its cracked spine starting to frazzle,
I'd sat with our Bible as well,

Leafing to where it parted
About the stiff bracts and flowers,

Locks of hair, clippings
The air still managed to yellow.

What was precious was held—thought
And breath, the vessel of the body.

Palms pressed together meant prayer,
Cupped meant water being lifted up.

A Poem Written for the Aviary at a Time of Its Possible Closing

Fabulous as the flowers
They preen among, the floating world
In which they come to rest

High in the hold of light,
They nest upon girders or wade
Through the waters of pools

Cloud-banked with shadows.
We find them choiring in branches,
In rookeries and dovecotes

Of the upturned ark of glass.
Because he has asked me,
I lift my young son up before

The condor's enormous darkness—
Its scruffy lei of feathers,
That head like a table scrap—

And feel his bones thrill
To be dangling there, fully
Within creation, as if heaven

Among us meant just such rooms.
Bernal Díaz thought as much,
Marching more than a mile into the sky

Above the New World,
Coming upon Tenochtitlán
Whose aviaries were brimming

With quetzals and macaws,
The hummingbirds, small jade
Blurs sipping nectars.

When Cortés burned the birds
Of paradise, their plumed flames
Drifted through the rubble

Of that sun, and the ashes
They would not be rising from,
Then or later, except as words

From this prayer spoken over water
In a place of wings
For creation's remnant flocks.

Ash and Stone

I

Poor parish: pallets stacked rotting
In the churchyard, a rose of Sharon

Seedling no one's bothered to pull
Growing through a crack in the slats,

Rain-streaked stone bearing its own
Gray weather. Inside, I find the angel

With the flaming sword still blazing
In a window of glittering, bright

Shards, the angel with the snowy
Wings still guarding a vacant tomb.

I recognize the chancel, that cup
I thought meant Blood of the Lamb,

The stone basin I was baptized in
By a man named Bliss. With no faith

But in the past's capacity to wound
And the wound's to heal, I kneel here

Where wafers wadded on my tongue,
My thirsty father guzzled his sips

Of wine beside me, and make my one
Confession to the altar, the walls

Of stone, before rising once more
To enter no life but my own,

And no world but the one I came in
From, moments ago.

II

One life is not
The only one. In Chiodo's,
Hanging from the pressed-tin tiles

Of the ceiling, what would otherwise
Be memory, or dust, or a pure floating
Stratum of the heavens, hovers

In its canopy above the bar: miners'
Hats and lanterns, harness bells
Near the sheer-spun mesh of nylons

Dangling in puckered rows. Old bras
Turned to rose. The sun's length
Of body in the dusk-colored coils

Of a dead snake packed in its oils . . .
And all of it glazed with time as with
The yellowing haze of a varnish

Through which the light has trailed
Its pollens. I think my father must
Have passed here more than once,

Trying to dodge his ghosts
A few blocks from the river,
The worn streets runged above him

Like lines left from the flood.
A new house and new wife and a life
Like a shoreline he believes he may

Never reach. Today, the whole town
Drowned in those waters,
I found shadows flooding the soap-

Clouded windows of the building
Where his office used to be,
The ark of the mills torn down.

III

There were days, my father told us,
When it got so bad he had to stop off

On the way to work and douse down
His nerves with a shot of vodka,

Limpid and gleaming as glycerin
Within the thick lens of the glass.

It evened things out, like a bleb
In a level. The bar would be empty,

Except for him, the first mill workers
Just drifting in from the graveyard

Shifts at U.S. Steel and Mesta,
The drowned light rising in mists

Off the river. Those were mornings,
He told us, when he'd find that light

In his mirror, dead as the metal
Behind its glass, a taste like blood

On his tongue, and only the one thing
For it that he ever found would work.

IV

On August 1, 1898, time just beginning
To tarnish its brick, like the sooty tars
Of smoke from the coke works and mills,

This branch of the library was opened,
LET THERE BE LIGHT
Chiseled into the lintel. My grandfather

Might have passed by here, Sundays,
During the seven years he had left
Before snapping his spine on the mill floor

When my father was nine months old.
If not for the twelve-hour shifts
They worked, seven days a week,

He could have come up these terraces
Under the branched globes of gas-lamps
And entered the elegant shelved rooms

Embellished with ivory and marble.
He could have strolled across
The quarter-sawn boards, in the hush

Of print and comfort, the ranked spines
Of books gathered in row after row,
And the grain in the polished oak.

Or, perhaps like Debs, he'd have cursed
Such "gifts from our slain comrades"
And gone to a tap-room instead.

Recently restored, historical
As the Carrie Furnaces across the river
In Rankin, it's empty today

Except for the fading light and carpets,
A smudged newspaper left out
Of its rack, already starting to yellow.

V

DEED.

THE

Homestead Cemetery
Company

TO

Robert Gibb

Lot 179c East Half

Section L

Price $20

Dated July 27 1900

VI

In the Homestead Cemetery, down
Across the slope from the cannon

Of the war memorial on which we used
To play, I stand staring at the name

Of my father, which is my own,
Cut into the final stone and light

Of the summer noon. I have had my
Entire life to get used to his silence,

And stand in it again today, finally
Without awkwardness. Now whatever

We say to one another, whatever
We fail to say, is all one with the light

And lack of wind, the mounds of dried
Flowers. Now that he is ash and stone.

The last time we sat alone together,
Father and son, the cold sky blank

With light, we barely spoke more than
Now. Already he was becoming one

Of a race of fathers from whom only
Silence comes. Now even the stones

Around us make more sound, sunlight
Ticking from them and the crumbling

Ovens of the mills. Whatever questions
I ask here, these are the answers he gives.

The Jars

This is an authentic "specimen" jar, used in the Section of Amphibians and Reptiles, Carnegie Museum of Natural History, from about 1900 to the 1930s.

Some specimens grown obsolescent
On their dreamy shelves, in the blown glass
Of jars they've been rinsed from since,
We stand among the clean, ranked cylinders
Which are being sold, here in the crowded
Workroom in the belly of the museum.
From here they'll be recast as "museum pieces"
Themselves, examples of the glass-maker's
Craft, or turned more likely into canisters
For spice racks, the small lidded urns
In which herbs are sealed. Into cruets
And decanters for oil. I've come looking
For a suitable terrarium, having promised
My son his own green swatch of planet

Breathing in its globe. I'd like to show him
This room where cold-blooded swimmers
Drift in vats grown faintly golden with
Their fats. Frogs with skins like grape leaves,
Coddled turtles, snakes wound snuggly
As hoses against the glass, their markings

Of leaf-mulch and shadow. I wish I could
Show him what dwells in gleaming rows
Among the bodies of the drowned, as though
This were the land of wonders, or the jars
Melville found filled with spermaceti
In which angels doused their hands.

Sifting through the Remains

I

I set them out before me: ring, bracelet, pin,
The ball-peen hammer someone helved
For my father, a few coppery coins—
Things handed down, taken up again.

Lifting his watch from the fraying case,
Something of time fills my palm
With the weight of a small still bird,
The inlaid wreath of tarnish staining its face.

In the lid I find my father's script—
From Helen, Xmas, 1929—and imagine
My mother's thin, gloved hand
Weighing choices at the jeweler's: onyx

Sets of pencils and gold-nibbed fountain
Pens, and on the shelves below
Them, the pocket watches berthed in rows,
Springs wound with the unsprung hours.

II

What did my mother number among her sins,
Fingering the forgiving wood?
What remains of her on the crucifix,
Where silver plate's worn thin,

But traces of her oils? Dark beads
And decades spilling from the vial
In which it's been kept, I think of her saying
This rosary, as though her body

Were filled with tongues eager
To speak, her breath to lend its sweetness
To the phrases. Again today I have only
The story of how she woke my father

In the dead of night, the desperate
Syllables rattling out, *now and in the hour,*
Till the priest salved unction upon her brow,
The cross dropped like a plummet.

III

And my father, alone now, did he also trace
The numb blear of beads through his fingers,
Staring into the hasps and roses
And that tiny savior's eroded face?

Is that why I never caught him handling it
Or saw the pages of this book they brought
From their wedding—a clutch of pale flowers,
Dates still to be filled? Why we never visited

Her grave? Better that brighter ceremony,
Vows echoing through the chancel, incense
From the censer drifting in grainy beams
Of light. Better them both, new to the body

They're forming, walking back up the aisle.
You can see it in photos of them entering
Their rooms, roses on the wallpaper glowing,
Their lives like the fur rippling on her stole.

Lost Waters

Because I am now the same age my mother was
The night she woke to the darkness
And told my father, *Call the priest, I'm dying,*

I look again into my hands and try to read a past
Which is so many dead ends and broken lines,
The grain checked through their seams.

Because I was only a bundle of milk and bone,
Chrisomed in the incubator when she was lowered
Into the earth, I unfacet the map and smooth it

On the table like a cloth, reading off the names
Of streets and the way they cluster toward her
Buried in the center of their maze.

Now that the years have also gone back
Into air and water, I spend the end of each day
Driving again through Homestead, past

The razed and gutted and fire-stormed stores,
Writing down what's vanished in the pages
Of the book I keep tucked in my breast pocket.

I take up her photos and stare at flesh
That underlies my own, pearls lit as the lamps
I've pictured flooding that room

In which they hauled me from her currents—
A scalpel like a sleek fish slicing me from
The thrumming of the only blood I'd known.

I'd like to drift downward once more,
As if swimming at night, leaving the maze and pages,
The pearls in their clusters like roe.

I'd like to pass among the dark braids
Rilling in those waters, my body pale as milt.
When she spilled open, flayed on the table below me,

I'd been pried through layers to find my voice
In a cold room buzzing with light, and have
Carried the world as no one before her could,

And would arrange my past as carefully
As the bones of her framed and even face.
Out of one life, one death—the terrible exchanges.

Salvation Army

Holidays, over their kettles, the bells
As if calling us to prayer, you'd see them,
Solemn and uniformed, soldiers of the faith,

Bound with the same cloth as their Bibles.
I'd thought they were the ones from the hymn,
Marching off, clothed in the whole armour.

They'd chastened me already, one summer
In vacation school, for dealing crazy eights
In the corner behind the blue upright piano.

"Devil's cards!" she'd actually shrieked.
You'd have thought we were casting lots,
Or profaning the calculus of heaven

With our sums. All summer we'd called out
Passages, chapter and verse, that we'd learned
By heart, counting off rolls of the children

Of Israel with the number of their names,
Marking the sons of Aaron and messengers
Of Job. We listed angels in their orders,

The ten commandments and seven lamps,
The multiplication of sorrows. I'd thought
The six-sided mesh of wire embedded

In those windows was a comb: honey out
Of the carcase, the way the light spilled
Through it, filling the room. Thirty sheets

And thirty change of garments. My mind
Swarmed with snatches of First Corinthians
And Second Kings, the book of generations,

Houses of clay crushed before the moth.
I called out in turn who it was could number
The clouds in wisdom, named the third river,

The fifth foundation of the city wall,
As though the whole world were in code,
Each hour a house marked for reassembly

Where rust became gold from the fire.
Each hour numbered by its appointed bell,
And nothing under heaven left to chance.

The Employments of Time in Homestead

All these families, the whole community that I knew,
was totally blasted . . . They weren't there anymore.
And so, that was the way that was, when I went back.
—THOMAS MCGRATH

"Where is home?"
—ROBERT CULP

1

According to the haphazard loom of heaven,
Or something in the air,

The mail gets shoved up under the brass flap
Of the slot anytime between morning

And the shadows of afternoon. I'll be done
At my desk or not, depending on the rhythms,

Then prowl through the rented rooms
Before walking out back to kneel among

The new green leaves of the garden,
Or, today, watching that mouse on the sidewalk

Scamper in circles like a mechanical toy,
Its bloodstream hopping with D-Con.

2

This is home in the loaned house in the city
Where I was born, north of the river

Whose rusts still tint the opening blossoms
Of the dogwood and bleed through the cast-off

Metals of scrap heaps and corroding sheds.
These days, down there, men can't even make

The living promised to the bread of their sweat.
It will take some time getting used to the dead

Gray light in Homestead, the mill shore as naked
As the shaved skin around a scar.

Time getting used to the Warsaw
Of boarded and burned-out stores,

Blocks of rubble where my father's office stood
And traffic stopped as the gates clanged down,

The great train of names on the boxcars
Came rumbling past.

3

There beneath his grasses my father's ashes
Quicken with the coming rains.

Today, the mills his father was killed in,
That his mother kept him from, are also graves

Filled with traces of metal, the ore yards
Are one long tomb. Here finally,

A century later, they're dedicating a plaque
In honor of the unmarked plots of those fallen

In Homestead when the Pinkertons attacked:
Handfuls of words being carried out

Over handfuls of earth . . . From up the slope
I catch snatches of that sermon

About sufferings and rust, lockouts, the seeds
Sown like ashes in dust or stony ground,

And how all of it, eventually,
Enters the new world for which they worked.

4

Because Fridays still mark the end of the week,
Whether there's work or not,

I head across the river to Chiodo's and listen
To lives whose dreams for the future

Fall to next year's teams. They waited here
For years for the mills to catch fire again,

Stacks massed like burning pillars,
For the sooty angels to ascend again

Into the furnaces of heaven. Waited
For the billowings of smoke from which

A still voice told them the dust had turned
To pollen, the iron been converted to steel,

There where slag heaps spilled their sunsets
From the lit rim of the world.

5

Today for my birthday my son gives me
The eight stapled pages of the book he's made

In which the boy plays baseball
And the father falls down, sweaty and tired,

At the end of a day of work. Shall I tell him
About the laid-off hosts I've sat with

Who would gladly collapse onto their bar-stools,
Rinsing the grit of metals from their throats

At the end of an eight-hour shift?
Or that I've found the only friend I grew up with

Who is still in town, and how, laboring
For Mesta until it closed, he spent

The next ten years replacing windshields,
Too bitter to have sons of his own?

6

In a world where work is sacramental
Shall I tell him how, on those immense nights

Before inspection, I swept the mill floor clean
With powdered cement, eight hours

At union scale sowing that pale floury chaff
Until the floor shone softly as a granary's,

Or the milky surface of a mill pond in which
The moon was drowned, and how I'd pause,

Leaning on my broom as if it were a pole,
And what loomed above me wasn't simply

Furnaces, but the actual machinery of heaven
In whose glory we were all employed.

A Memorium for the Syria Mosque Razed to Make Space for Parking

Listen, you could hear the flesh
Dampering its octaves along the neck
Of the guitar clear up in the balcony
Where I sat, thinking of shoes
On a freshly waxed floor, the wood

Stage gleaming, the polished brass
Molten once more, and the bell
Of the vault above us lit with sound.
You could feel the surge of music,
A tide which lifted the whole mosque

Clear of time. I remember the scallop
Of lines, seats red as fezzes
On which the curved swords glowed,
How outside, snug against the eaves,
Tiles patterned the walls in a fret—

A little band of color, beadwork
Against that naked expanse.
And the bare breasts of the sphinxes flanking
The stairs, as though the dark bronze
Of honey poured in their forms.

Martha in Darkness

Solstice: a cold brass flatness of sun
Halfway along the river where my aunt,
Widowed and losing sight,

Sorts through the shadows that spill
Into her rooms. If old age were a meadow,
This would be late fires burning

Through ground fog. Instead, it is a house
Slowly turning into memory and Braille.
A bad time, she tells us, her bones

Grown so frail they feel like shells,
Porous and worn thin. *Bone china,*
I remember, my stepmother and her

Together, holding the glazed plates
Up to light. Today the sky looks like that,
Overcast and snowing, evening

Coming on. In the window beyond her,
The bare thatch of the privet glistens
Against the sidewalk. I think of her,

Large in her bra and girdle, startled
By my sudden appearance on the stairs,
This woman who is now only sticks.

Those years, come fall, I'd follow her
From the cellar, carrying the brandy-soaked
Ball of mincemeat she'd swaddle

With dough. She showed me how clouds
Cooled my cup. Today, she'll see nothing
But the soft, blurred shapes

Of her furniture, walls which deepen
Into shade between the dim-lit panes.
Even Emsworth, in places, is grown

More indistinct, and our faces before her.
When my cousin leaves the room,
She sighs, "A son is not a husband,"

And then wonders again if I remember
Waking in bed in that warm cocoon
Between her and my Uncle Gran.

II

Magnetic North

I

The scale of the machine those nights,
Hard above us like the sky: one weld
And then another where fire poured

Into shapes, the great sheds vast
As hangars placed end to end,
Cranes in the rigging of their girders.

Three miles of the river. Three shifts
In which to raise up Leviathan,
Daily, from tons of battered earth.

Common labor or millwright, you could
Feel heat shimmering on your face
Twenty feet from the ovens, see

Loose flakes dancing upon the backs
Of slabs. You could watch as almost
Molten metals were being rolled

Into finished lengths of plate.
Everything there fed the flames
Except what came burning from them,

The night sky glittering like a coal seam,
Blast furnaces and open hearths
Glowering through clouds of smoke.

"Metal from Heaven," the Sumerians
Called iron, meteoric, fallen to earth.
In Homestead it was ore, oxides or salts

Of the metal, or sintered out of pig.
It was steel when you added carbon
And were ready to tap the heat.

II

As though the past were a landscape
I could walk through, just by being
Where it took place, I keep expecting

To find Joe Derry's father at his post
In front of First Federal, blind face
Shining above the till of his cigar box

And cup filled with sharpened pencils.
Where, around the corner from him
On Amity Street, steelworkers still pass

Beneath the banner of the gate and on
Into the tabernacles, the great sheds
In which my grandfather plunged

Like an angel, his body broken
And on fire. I keep thinking I'll find
Trolleys shuttling beneath the ozone

That singes their sky, ore yards, cigar
Cars rattling on the Hot Metal Bridge.
Yesterday I even searched for hours

In the face of a man, grown sallow-
Skinned and balding, for the friend
I used to know, and never found him.

What happened to the high school
In which we jostled against each other
Because a world was beginning

Just for us? The Leona Theater,
In whose arced, voluptuous darkness
Curtains parted for us like the sea?

III

I used to lean my back there against
A corrugated wall which now is only
A rippling in the light, face the river,

And eat my lunch at 4 A.M., mill fires
Ruddying the skies. I'd watch as red
Shifts of tail-lights angled north

Across the continuous truss
And trestles of the High Level Bridge,
Eager to join them, then did.

Now, row homes and sidewalks
Buckling on the hill, Homestead's still
The most magnetic of my norths,

Though it's hard even to pass among
The ruins of Seventh Avenue, houses
Halved at their wallpaper, side lots

Strewn with rubble, or sit listening
To talk about jerry-built jobs
That steelworkers cobbled together,

Good weeks when they found some—
The mills left to the rats at last
And blood-hued lupus of rust,

Winds which empty through the weedy
Flats there along the river:
Full circle from when they plowed

The old wards under in 1941,
Making way for the expanding plant
And coming post-war boom.

IV

Now Snow's Tavern is gone,
Where I savored those first, froth-topped
Drafts at midnight after work,

And the trolley island I waited upon
For the last car up to the Park.
They tore down St. Mark's Chapel,

The "rooster church" whose weather-
Vane greeted the morning star.
Marks Card Shop is empty, in which

We'd ogled like the elders at Susanna,
Peeking through a stand of magazines
At the sleek breasts of the early '60s.

Woolworth's closed, then Grant's
Where flocks of canaries were caged
Against the ceiling—a dime-store

Quadratura bright with vaults of song.
Even WAMO's gone from the valley
Whose radios pulsed those nights

With the Moonglows and Five Satins,
The Flamingos' plangent shimmer
In "I Only Have Eyes for You."

The post office my Uncle Arch ran,
Heraldic among ink pads and stamps,
Has become the local lock-up.

The *Daily Messenger* caught fire,
Rending our past into mangled type
And the drenched stench of ashes.

The Big Shop shut down. Number
One Structural. Open Hearth Five.
Mills in which my grandfather died.

V

MANNER OF ROBERT GIBB'S DEATH

Former Johnstowner Broke His Neck in Fall at Homestead Mill on Saturday Afternoon.

Robert Gibb, whose sudden death on Saturday afternoon at the Homestead mills was announced in this paper that evening, was adjusting a belt in the Carnegie machine shop when he lost his balance and fell from a platform a distance of twenty-five feet. He fell on an iron casting and broke his neck, dying almost instantly.

Robert Gibb was thirty-five years of age and had been living in Homestead for the past twenty-two years. He is survived by his wife and three children. The deceased was a charter member of Mandala Lodge, No. 991, I.O.O.F., of Homestead, having served the order in all its offices. Mr. Gibb was a sober and industrious citizen and a kind and loving husband and father. He was highly esteemed and his many friends were greatly shocked on learning of his untimely death.

VI

New Year's Eve: the last great cell
Of steel mills being felled, ridge-vents
Collapsing like shattered spines

Alongside the bridge I could have
Stepped from, any night of that life,
To walk out across the winged roofs

Shaped from the flames. I could have
Stayed up there, small and unnoticed
Above the ceaseless roar, searching

The struts until I stood above the spot
My grandfather dropped from,
Plummeting to the fire-seamed concrete

Of the floor. Or simply have nestled
Beside the sleeping birds, to wake
The next morning with domes

Of churches burning in my sight,
The whole valley molten, and done
My one stiff dance to rouse the blood,

Hopping from one leg to the next,
Cuffing my arms across my chest,
As though fully fledged at last.

Lewis Hine: Two Photographs

1. *The Puddler*

Posed like a pool player over his shot,
Features flooded at the oven door, the cue-
Length rabble prodding slag that's tapped
Each heat out through the cinder notch . . .

Not only the subject, which is signature,
But the handling of light boiling from
The spongy iron, makes the little tag,
Photo by Hine, redundant. Who else

Has been down there, head bowed above
The shuttered world, lens set to the fire?
There, where heat's simply another
Element, Hine's is the mixture of light

And time in which his figures are fixed
In emulsion. Like "coming to nature,"
As the puddler would say, the churned mass
Starting to harden. And isn't it by now

Second nature to them both, that flash
Of combustible metal—silver halide
Or manganese—at work on the world
They render from the material at hand?

2. *Washing at the Bosh*

Stripped to the waist and bathed in light
So physical the flesh seems compacted of it,
He bends above the bosh, washing his hands
Which are gleaming and black with grease.

An open faucet in the foreground.
Steam wisping against the gradual opacity
Of the mills: depths in a depth of field
The photographer's been staring into.

His point here—that workers washed
In the same waters in which they cooled
Their tools—has become over time almost
Incidental to the beauty of his photograph,

As has the aesthetic of protest and fact
That underlies it, though without them
We'd never have seen that luminous ingot
Of a body, or thought about Hine, finished,

Coming out the gate as the last ignitions
Of sunset erupt above the stacks, the trough
Of a river in which the mills seem cast
As in the dark mineral waters of the bosh.

Steel Engravings

1. *Slag Banks*

Nightly you'd see it, halfway up the sky,
That fissure of fire where the ladle cars
Tipped over, stoking the smoldering banks,
And below, where the glass of the river
Cast it back. Slag was what you were left with
When those fierce winds fled the ovens:

A breath hot as God's which melted metal,
Welled flux to the furnace top. Six times
A day they drew slag off—twice each shift—
To buckle in hills stark as stricken Isaiah.
You'd see it burning above Nine-Mile Run
When the hinged cars clattered on the tracks.

In the beginning the planet cooled like that,
A mantle floating upon the molten core.
Slag was our horizon ringed with fire.

2. *Steel Blooms*

When ingots got lifted out of those pits
In which they'd been soaking up heat
And were broken, glowing, into sections,
One ton each, then we said steel had turned
Into *blooms,* the air about them flowering
Like light at the red end of the spectrum.

The whole mill seemed to be flourishing
Within the blush of that florescence
When we rolled them into rails: bright
Streaming ribbons, solid lengths of fire
We knew the world would soon travel
By twos over ties and gravel roadbeds.

Hot saw, we said, cutting lengths. *Chill*
And *annealing. Grooving the mill,* when it
All went well. *Cupola* and *case* and *pulpit.*

3. *Pig Iron*

Not, as I'd thought, owing to the crudeness
Of a metal fed with scrap, or because
It was rendered from the animal, the hocks
And hams compacted above its trotters,
The dark, gristly chambers of the heart.
And not because, like Latin, it was polyglot.

In the early furnaces they poured iron off
Into casting beds—each mold attached
To the other like pigs suckling at the sow.
Energy meant mass. Chimneys the size
Of brick-kilns, skips in which they charged
The stock. The belled dome of the hopper.

There were shifts when you were on the tit.
There were shifts when you did better
To remember the farrow eaten by their sow.

Quatrains for a Christmas Bear

I

Black and massive as an upturned stump,
It rummaged among us, this December,
Ravenous for rinds and the sour mash
In trash cans set out in city yards,

And managed to sleep it off, unnoticed
In whatever covert it found:
A quarter ton of slumbering earth
Alert to the faintest of sounds.

It must have come up through the woods
From Duck Hollow and the Monongahela,
Following the clear spoor of winter stars
To where they grew tangled and lost

Within the general heaven of arc lamps
And headlights on passing cars.
Three days and nights, like a story,
Or the passage of a tragic god.

II

Nearing the solstice it was seen once more,
Dogged by wardens and the competing
Cameras from the evening news,
But now on the far shore of the river,

Hunched and coaly as the foothills
Rising beyond the old mill towns.
And whether because the wilderness
Brushed against us like a scent

Or because my own loneliness was salved,
I like to imagine its slow withdrawal,
Ambling in shadow across an empty bridge,
Or swimming that distance,

Snout lifted above the iron cold chop
Of those waters, breath on the air—
A bear the color of the winter night,
Companions above it, constellated there.

For the Inmate Pedro Velázquez, Who Restored a Wooden Tricycle for Our Youngest Son's Christmas

Laving the red enamel so lovingly
The brushstroke left no wake,

Did you also loose yourself
From the cell-blocks and vanish into time?

Did the balm of clear wood calm you?
The bearings steeping in their oil?

I picture the tricycle spread before you
Like a diagram, all parts, your hands

As they move about them, carefully
As though parsing out powder,

The plush tongue of the candle
Blackening the bottom of its spoon . . .

But what interests me this morning
Is the light I imagine flooding

The prison workshop and your intent
Lone figure, illuminating the wheels

And washers, the tiny crosses
In the domes of Phillips-head screws.

I know it is only the cold fluorescence
Breaking from the long tubes

Banked above you, casting each detail
Into sharp-edged relief: the still,

Forged metals, your soiled thumbnail
Split lengthwise into its quick.

I know it is not the glare of heaven
Or arrangement in idealized space

Such as the painter Velázquez glazed,
Filling the stalls of his street scenes

Until the ordinary shook with grace.
I know, but still it falls upon you

Like your own painstaking shimmer,
Flawless as water below the lifted brush.

Phipps Conservatory

A dirigible of a building,
It floats above the lily ponds
And gardens, the long swale of lawns
Across which shadows are passing
Like summer clouds.

I came here often, growing up,
With my sketch-pads and paints,
Trying to render pencil trees,
The flaming bird of paradise,
As if such attention

Were an act of faith.
I sketched in the almost
Ottoman scrolls of its roofs,
The spidery lattices in which glass panes
Hovered like squares of light,

There above the fronds
Of date palms: a green world
Far removed from the flower-scented tissues
My Aunt Hettie kept in her purse,
The smothering bouquets

Of funerals, the neutered ones
From church. Here even the names
Seemed wild, bear grass bristling,
Snake cactus writhing on its roots.
Today, it is the sight

Of the cocoa-shade's
Plush red vulva that soothes me,
The delicate petals on the slender
Buddha's lamp. In a room where orchids
Loll about their pollens,

I watch fronds change to fish
In a pond. And in the grotto,
Underneath the sea-hibiscus and satinwood,
I find where I leaned against her,
Aching to ease the zipper

Further down her front
That she might spill gleaming
As if from a tree. Or I might reach
Into the brightness. Behind us, tiers of moss
And lichen spread

From the rank clefts of the stones.
What do plants remember?
Or flesh? I run my hand along the wall,
While outside, in the courtyard, the bonsai deepen
In their twisty sprawl.

First Visit to My Mother's Grave, North Side Catholic Cemetery

How are the dead raised up?
—I CORINTHIANS 15:20

Here not even one tree, empress or ailanthus,
Shelters the industrial dirt and hardpan
That make up the ground, plots laid out
Like subdivisions in small, adjoining tracts.

Not even a stone's above her head or set down
At her feet, or small swale settled in
The burning earth to show just where she lies.
In the thin leaves of "The Burial of the Dead"

It says *the sun shall not burn thee by day,*
But the only shade here is the one I've brought
With me among the stiff, dry thatch of grasses
Swirling across the hills. In the whole

Half plot the stone of her grandfather weathers
The light alone. Or so I thought, until the grave-
Digger showed and began testing the ground
For markers and old plaques toppled with time.

To have to dig for her like that, taking turns
Ripping up mats of droughty sod, the crimped
Blade clanging, when all we'd find were names
From another century nearly worn away.

To have come all this way only to find one more
Absence to stand before, like the sad graves
Of the river. Just south of here the world
We shared for twenty days has nearly vanished—

The sun's dark furnace burning above the mills,
The furnaces of night we heard roaring beneath
The earth. The night the blood burst in her brain
I heard only the sound of the great sea

Slurring around me where I lay, swaddled
In the incubator, the blood-rose umbilical
Knotted off. She was the first of my losses,
labour and sorrow, short her *threescore years*

and ten. She was the one flesh of the body
My flesh came from, *the grass of the morning*
cut down and dried up. The dead are raised up
In sorrow, and in language alone.

Cigar: An Ode

Call the roller of big cigars
—WALLACE STEVENS

1.

Even now they're sitting in Bloom's
On the threadbare chairs, South-Side
Cognoscenti, opulent among clouds

Of smoke, while piled about them
In boxes and blocks, the humidor's
Beveled shelves, cigars lie arrayed

In sizes and shapes, the racked hue
Of leaves in which they're wrapped,
Each bound with the crest of its band.

2.

I'd sport such a ring, evenings
I sat transfixed in the living room
By Uncle Arch, watching him roll

A *Punch Habana* before the blue flame
Of his match, intoning tobacco
In small quick puffs as the lit end

Caught and coaled, and I could watch
The faint white rime of ashes
Taking hold, like a papery spume.

Even now I see him in sepia, light
Falling through the lamp shade where
They found him dead in that chair,

Slumped as though fallen asleep
Above the paper he was reading,
Cigar in the ash-tray, grown cold.

3.

"Durable fire," Raleigh called them.
This one's the color of ground coffee,
Ring-finger thick, rich as a portobello.

My son loves the smell, he tells me,
And the paraphernalia—matchbook
And clipper, the hinged, exotic box—

And the way we are gathered together
In the space through which that slow
And flameless corona continues to burn.

4.

Cigar, because in Cuba *cigarral* meant
Tobacco nursery or summer-house.
And what of those rollers in the *cheruta*'s

High, windowed room? What news were
They being read that day, bent above
Their knives and flat stacks of tobacco,

The lector on his platform before them,
Unfaceting the morning's paper,
Snapping open the awkward folds?

Folding the Fox

My oldest son, discovering numbers
And the laws of structure in the crystal's walls,
The gray comb woven in the wasp's nest,
Comes to me this evening bearing a sheaf
Of paper and the book in which the ancient art
Lies charted, the animals are creased into being.
Together we practice intricacies of wing fold
And crimp fold, water bomb base, learning
To master the basic emergence of shapes.
My son turns out cups like lilies and those
Severe white birds, almost Egyptian
In their beauty, while I finally muster up
A squash fold from the welter of worn,

Misguided pleats, recalling the simpler veer
Of airplanes tossed into flight, the kites
I boxed together like cartons of light.
When I was nine, my Uncle Arch taught me
How to knot a tie, standing behind me
In the mirror, kind hands on mine fashioning
The loops of fabric and drawing them tight.
Now, tonight, I try to guide hands which ache
To vanish among the crisp divisions
Of paper, as together we follow the fox
Through petal and bird base, five-sided square,
To where the flame-shaped tail plumes
Before us across newly emblazoned air.

The Burning World

I

The great slabbed stairways mounting
To the dead level of the lot,
It looks almost Toltec, pyramidal

And squared by its block of streets.
I have to imagine the high school,
Gone now for decades, the dingy brick

And masonry, and a boredom so immense
Even the hours seemed made of stone.
The rain letting up, I park my car

And step across the unsettling grid
Of concrete fissuring now with weeds,
The scraggly stands of sumac

In groups like teenaged girls.
I wish I remembered them better,
The years we spent together here

Amid clanking pipes and blackboards
While dense banks of clouds over Asia
Began to fling their jellied fires.

I wish I remembered the names,
Now that none of it is left, not even
The lavatories filled with our smoke,

The rain-filled panes of our mirrors,
Mills and machine shops into whose
Furnaces we passed. I wish I'd searched

The windows more for some glimmer
Of the world I'd be entering today,
The last waters pouring off into storm

Mains and gutters, flushing the veins
Of Gloria Grib clean of what killed her,
Who I knew once, and mourn.

II

Because trees were summer nights
Redolent of rain, and breasts
Pale as the gleaming which lay

Just inside their bark, I look for
The bandstand and find it wreathed
As well with the dusk it stands in,

Alone from everything else
In Homestead, filigree weathered,
Paint flaking in an idle drift

Of motes. I waited here, evenings
One summer, feeling it fill with
Moonlight like a luminous room,

The moths floating dimly about me,
Mill smoke rising from the valley
Floor. I loved its fussy, eight-

Sided elegance, the fitted boards
That framed out the roof. Loved
Even the last grains of the dusk

In which I waited, watching paint
Take on the mauve of those tissues
She stuffed into her bras.

III

The Monongahela is green this morning,
The color of verdigris,
Or the pale lime of the railings

Flaking the length of the bridge.
Mists drift among the sallows.
A single barge plows upriver,

White wake feathering from its prow.
When we trolled down there, above
The carp and other bottom feeders,

Green meant only seepage and run-off
From the pipes, waters no one
Rose from or even fished to eat.

And yet I used to dream of them
Climbing into heaven nightly above
Their banks, the tops of trees swaying

Like saw grass under flood.
In them I'd find myself singing over
Rooftops, the ridged heaps of slag,

Watching as one source poured
Onto another, the scale of light
Across whatever current the darkness

Was rising into. I'd say my name,
Counting the pale syllables as they
Eddied past the mills, then spilled

Into the confluence, downtown
Where the old skyscrapers hovered
Like stanchions of a bridge,

The waters lit with everything
That bore me—fish, boat, or coal-star—
Choiring above those shores.

IV

The night that my mother woke alone
In the darkness, only to become a part
Of the dark, the lights must have

Remained lit in the small rooms
Of that house, the porch lamp with its
Wreath of wings, long after the priest

Had come and gone, and workers from
The funeral home. So, weeks later, what
Dear daughter lifted me from the incubator

As though it were a boat of rushes,
Bundling me home from the hospital
To my place in the burning world?

V

Helen F. Gibb

Age. 42 yrs

Died. Homestead Boro

Cause. Cerebral Embolis

Sept. 28th 1946

Lot 280 Sec. B # 6

Aug & Val Freinstein Lot—

Johnson Vlt. $35— } P a i d
L. Device 5— }

Gillen and Coulter

VI

Even the aluminum siding is sun-struck
And worn on the house on Sixteenth
Avenue, where I was born, and my father

Before me. The faded white of the dish-
Cloth his mother flung across his face
The year before he brought my mother

Home. The nominal white of the bone,
Or the pickets in this fence, ghosting
Back into a grain like driftwood's.

I woke here one night screaming that
Lucifer was under my bed, and found
His horned red head on the doorknob,

That Halloween, blocking my way
From the room. Those afternoons, when
I was three, my stepmother set a chair

In front of the kitchen window
So I might see the alley fill with children
On their way home from school.

All year I watched them as they passed—
Some running, some quiet as light.
Then, moments later, I'd watch again

As that boy went by on a leg which meant
Polio, which marked him as one
Who would inherit the world of his fathers

Already frozen in place. In that scuffling
His body spoke with a voice so bent
I heard it in my bones, telling me

Somehow, even then, that there were
Places we only reach by lurching,
Places we reach which stagger our lives.

Rust Belt

Perhaps you've passed him on the Rankin Bridge,
Heading back from the scrap yard in Braddock—
The slow child of the boroughs, retarded at birth.

He's steadily peddling, waving you by, tricycle bin
Emptied of its stash: cans and copper piping,
Bright compacted balls of foil. Seven A.M. and he's been

At work for an hour now, fog slowly burning off
The river where great carp lurk, the color
Of sunken brass. He'd salvage them too if he could,

Wring a few bucks extra these days when a good
Haul means aluminum at thirty cents a pound
And a bike that doesn't break down freighting it.

Scrap's hard to find now that Park Corporation
Has picked things clean. Dawn-to-dusk shifts
He's out there, in whatever kind of weather,

Checking Lapko's and Chiodo's bars, the lot
Next to Shop 'n Save. A good day means his jacket,
Gregory's Scrapping like stitched light flashing

From its satin on the local roads. The sun's braid
Crowns the horizon, and everywhere he looks
There's metal, the leaf of its rust turned to gold.

Homestead Park

April 1956 and my father
Is wearing his suede jacket
And short-brimmed hat.
We are going for a walk.
The joints of the willows
Are budding, the sumacs
Already have that smell

Like old paint in a can.
Though I am only ten
I notice that his shoes
Are just the same as those
He wears to work, only scuffed-up
And older. He is telling me
About my mother

Coming from the garden,
Ravenous and laughing,
The high sky brilliant with light.
I think about the office
Where he works, humming
With its great white refrigerators,
Freezers opened

On displays of plastic food.
Because I am only ten
The world is as it should be.
My father's jacket is brown
As his shoes, the under-bark
Of the sycamores soft green.
When my father tells me

The names of the trees
And the meanings of the terms
He uses, I can almost hear the rocks speak,
Jutting from the woods above us,
Covered with their words.
In my dreams the shadow
Of the valley runs down here

Along the edge of the creek,
But today, bright Saturday,
With my father beside me
The sky spreads its branches.
The woods go back as far
As our house. Everyone I know
Is still alive.

NOTES

"In the Emergency Room": The painting alluded to is Mantegna's *The Lamentation*, c. 1490–1500.

"A Poem for the Pittsburgh Aviary at the Time of Its Possible Closing": Bernal Díaz's account of the sacking of Tenochtitlán and the burning of its aviaries can be found in his *True History of the Conquest of New Spain.*

"A Memorium for the Syria Mosque Razed to Make Space for Parking": Despite efforts to preserve it, the Shriners' mosque was demolished in 1996.

"Ash and Stone": Eugene Debs's scornful remark (cited in section IV) was a reminder that Carnegie's libraries were financed by a fortune made through the labor of others, including those steelworkers who died providing it.

"The Employments of Time in Homestead": The "fallen" in section 3 are the "Homestead martyrs," the seven millworkers killed by Pinkertons in the famous Homestead Strike of 1892.

"Magnetic North": *Quadratura* (section IV) is the term for a kind of illusionist mural painting which features architectural details.

"Cigar: An Ode": In Cuba, the building in which cigars are made is called a *cheruta.* Traditionally, workers were read to by a lector, paid for that purpose. Readings varied throughout the day from novels to, as is here imagined, the local newspaper.

"Rust Belt": Park Corporation, an industrial salvager, bought and "developed" the property that had been the

Homestead Works of United States Steel. Part of that property (Homestead's old First and Second Wards) had been appropriated by the government in 1941 for the expansion of the mills. Many thought the land should have been returned to the town.